The European Capitals

A beautiful book introducing all the capitals from the countries inside the geographical limits of Europe. The geographical limits of Europe are the Atlantic Ocean to the West, and the Arctic Ocean to the North, the Mediterranean sea to the South and the Caucasus Mountains, the Ural River, the Caspian Sea, the Black Sea and the Turkish Straits to the East.

You can find all this information on our website at http://capitalsofgeographicaleurope.com/

List of the European capital:

Amsterdam, Andorra la Vella, Ankara, Athens, Baku, Belgrade, Berlin, Bern, Bratislava, Brussels, Bucharest, Budapest, Chisinau, Copenhagen, Dublin, Helsinki, Kyiv (also known as Kiev), Lisbon, Ljubljana, London, Luxembourg (city), Madrid, Minsk, Monaco, Moscow, Nicosia, Nur-Sultan, Oslo, Paris, Podgorica, Prague, Pristina, Reykjavik, Riga, Rome, San Marino, Sarajevo, Skopje, Sofia, Stockholm, Tallinn, Tbilisi, Tirana, Vaduz, Valletta, Vatican City, Vienna, Vilnius, Warsaw, Yerevan, Zagreb

Amsterdam

Netherlands' capital, it is known for its artistic heritage like the Van Gogh Museum and the Rijksmuseum. It has an elaborate canal system, numerous bike paths and narrow houses with gabled facades, legacies of the city's 17th-century Golden Age.

Andorra la Vella

Capital of Andorra, it is situated in the Pyrenees mountains between France and Spain. The 12th-century Sant Esteve church has baroque altarpieces and it is known as a duty-free retail hub. The elevation is 1,023 m for a population of around 22,000 thousand people.

Ankara

Turkey's capital sits in the country's central Anatolia region. Overlooking the city is Anitkabir, The big building overlooking the city is Anitkabir, the mausoleum of Kemal Atatürk. The capital is an altitude of 938 m and it has a population of around 5.4millins people.

Athens

Capital of Greece, it was also at the heart of Ancient Greece, a powerful civilization and empire. The city is still dominated by 5th-century BC landmarks, including the Acropolis, a hilltop citadel topped with ancient buildings like the collonaded Parthenon temple. It has a population of around 660,000 people and is situated at sea level.

Baku

Capital of Azerbaijan, Baku is famous for the Palace of the Shirvanshahs and the iconic stone Maiden Tower. The modern landmarks include the Heydar Aliyev Center and the flame towers. The city is situated along the Caspian Sea, altitude-28m, and it has a population of around 2 million people.

Belgrade

Capital of Serbia, Belgrade is situated at the confluence of the Danube and the Sara rivers. There is an important fort the Beogradska Tvrđava which dates back to the Roman time. It has a population of 1.3 million people.

Berlin

It is the capital of Germany with around 4 million people. It is famous for modern art and the wall which separated the city in two during the cold war.

Bern

Capital of Switzerland, it is also known as the federal city. It is famous for its historical centre.

Bratislava

Capital of Slovakia, it is situated on the Danube at the border with Austria. It is famous for its vineyard, its castle and the little Carpathian mountain. It has a population of around 400,000 people.

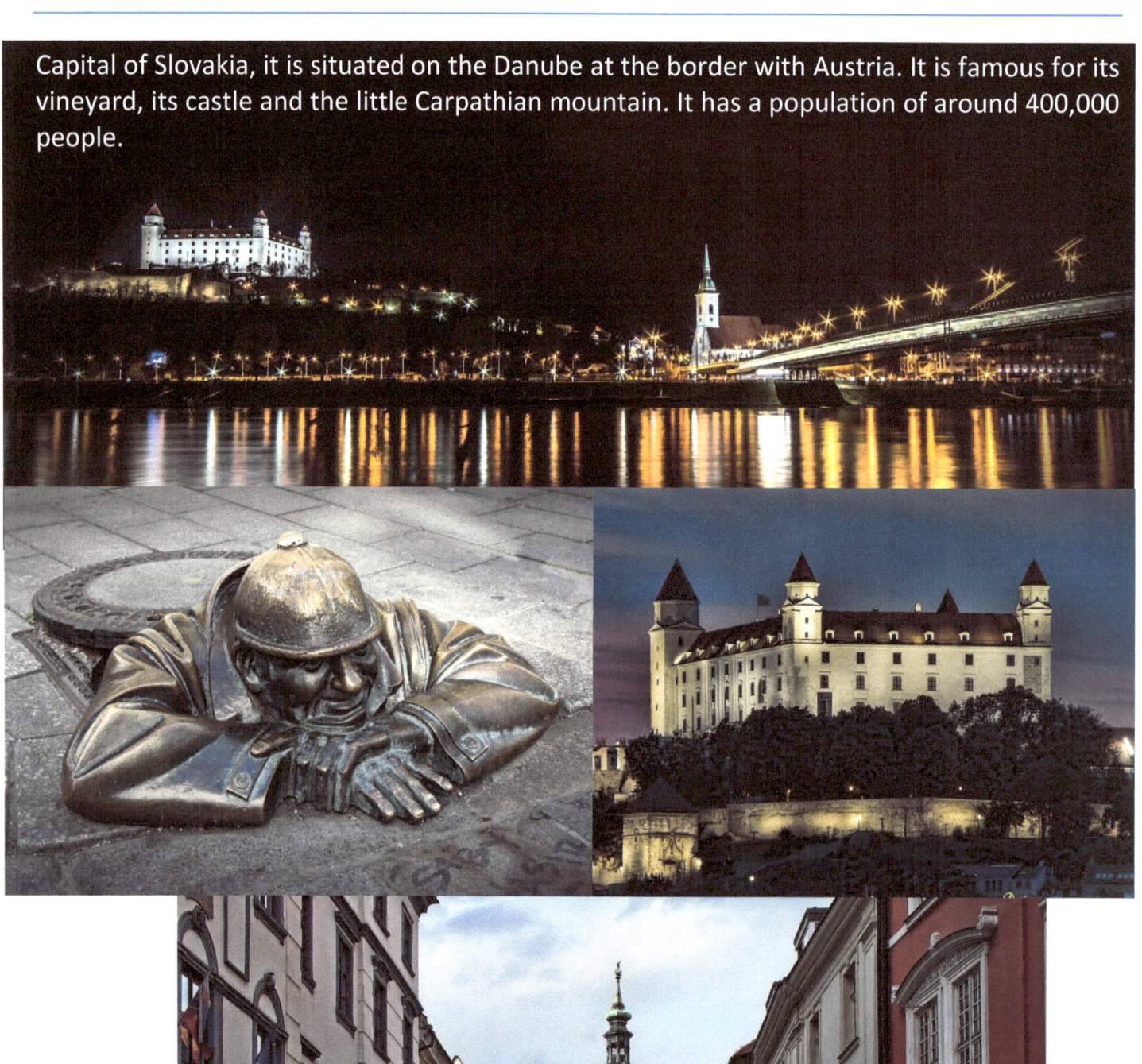

Brussels

Capital of Belgium, It is famous for its Manneken pis, atoms and old buildings. It has a population of 1.1million people.

Bucharest

Capital of Romania, it has a population of 1.8 million people, it is famous for an iconic historic centre and a massive building from the communist era, the Palatul Parlamentului

Budapest

Capital of Hungary, it is a city along the Danube famous for its bath and its parliament. It is home to 1.7 million people.

Chisinau

Capital of Moldova, it is famous for its Cathedral in the city centre. It has a population of 600,000 people.

Copenhagen

Denmark's capital, it is famous for the little mermaid, the colourful houses, the historic centre and their royal family.

Dublin

Capital of the Republic of Ireland, it is famous for its beer, its historic centre and its temple bar.

Helsinki

Finland's capital, Helsinki is famous for its main street, Mannerheimintie. It has a population of around 600,000 people.

Kyiv

Kyiv or Kiev, it is the capital of Ukraine. Kyiv is famous for its cathedral, Maidan square and the orthodox churches. There are nearly 3 million people in Kyiv.

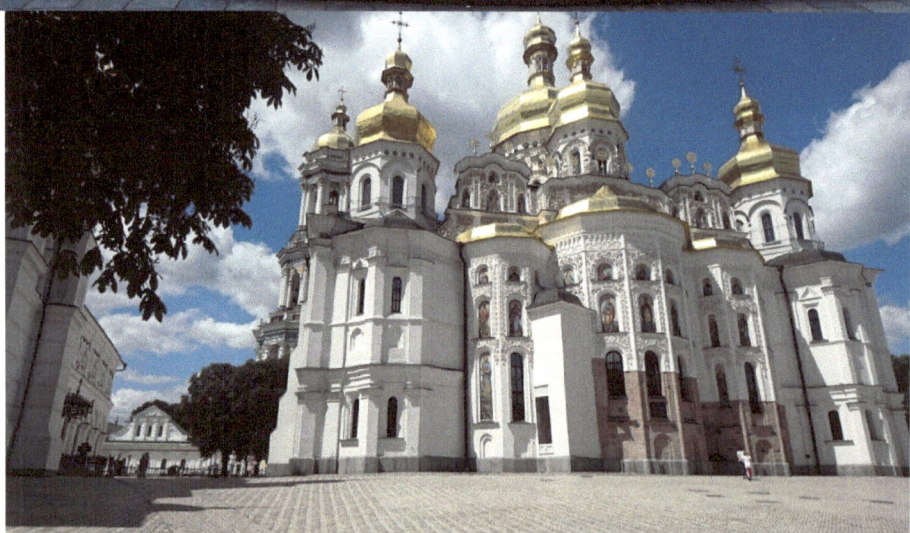

Lisbon

Portugal's coastal capital, it is famous for the Tower of Belem and the wonderful city centre including the Praça do Comércio. There are half a million people in Lisbon.

Ljubljana

The largest city and capital of Slovenia, Ljubljana is famous for its university, castle and green spaces.

London

Capital of the United Kingdom, It is famous for its buildings, royal family and its buses. There are a bit more than 8 million people living in London.

Luxembourg

Capital of Luxembourg, it is famous for its historical city centre with a population of around half a million people. It is also famous for being a small country between France, Belgium and Germany.

Madrid

Capital of Spain, Madrid is famous for its beautiful boulevards and avenues, its football team, small streets with delicious tapas bars and the museum del Padro. Around 3 million people lived in Madrid.

Minsk

Capital of Belarus, it is famous for its city centre, its art scene and the red church.

Monaco

It is a city-state, famous for its casinos, Grand Prix motor race and expensive lifestyle.

Moscow

Capital of Russia, with 13 million people, it is a busy capital. It is famous for its red square and churches.

Nicosia

Capital of Cyprus, it is divided in two, the northern part is in the Turkish part of the Turkish side of Cyprus and the southern part of the capital is in the other Cyprus.

Nur-Sultan

Previously known as Astana, it is the capital of Kazakhstan. There are around 1 million people in Nur-Sultan and the city is famous for its mosque and skyscraper.

Oslo

Capital of Norway, the city s famous for the Vikings living there and the museums in the city. A bit more than half a million people live there.

Paris

City of lights and the capital of France, it is a wonderful city famous for its historical city centre and gastronomy.

Podgorica

Capital of Montenegro, it is famous for its bridge and rivers. It also has a wonderful historical centre. A bit less than 200,000 people live there.

Prague

Capital of the Czech Republic, it is famous for its Old Town Square and historical building. Around 1.2 million people live there.

Pristina

Capital of Kosovo, it is a delicate one because Kosovo is not recognised by every country in the world.

Reykjavik

Capital of Iceland, it is a beautiful city famous for its Viking origin, its harsh weather, nature and the northern lights.

Riga

Capital of Latvia, it is famous for its old city centre, its market and its canals.

Rome

The eternal city, capital of Italy, it is famous for being the capital of the Roman Empire. It has wonderful monuments and restaurants.

San Marino

Oldest republic known to date, this small country is situated in the northeast of Italy. It is also famous for its castle on top of the rock.

Sarajevo

Capital of Bosnia and Herzegovina, it is famous for its historical city centre and the mountains surrounding the city.

Skopje

Capital of North Macedonia, it was mainly a Muslim city until the XIXth century. It is famous for the Kale fortress.

Sofia

Capital of Bulgaria, for thousands of years it has been at the centre of the Balkan peninsula. It is at the foot of the ski mountain Vitosha. 1.2 million people live in Sofia.

Stockholm

Capital of Sweden, nearly 1 million people live there. This coastal city was founded 8,000 years ago.

Tallinn

Capital of Estonia, it is famous for looking like a doll city. The city centre is well preserved and around 400 thousands people live there.

Tbilisi

Capital of Georgia, Tbilisi has lovely buildings like modern and traditional building. In summer, a small river, flowing down the city, cool down the 1.5 million people living there.

Tirana

Capital of the Republic of Albania, it is surrounded by mountains and it is famous for its parks. Around 610,000 people enjoy Tirana mild Mediterranean weather.

Vaduz

Capital of Liechtenstein, only around 5 thousands people live there. It is famous for its castle and for being a small capital in the middle of the Alps.

Valletta

Capital of Malta, nearly 400,000 people live there, maybe more in summer. The city itself looks like a fortress.

Vatican city

A small city-state within Rome, it is famous for being the city of the Holy Church and the pope. There are around 1000 people living there.

Vienna

Capital of Austria, one of the best to live in the world, it is Vienna. The city has a beautiful and historical city centre with a not so much polluted air.

Vilnius

Capital of Lithuania, around 700, 000 people live there and it is famous for its historical city centre, the Old Town has around 2,000 buildings of historical importance.

Warsaw

Capital of Poland, the city itself is a lovely mix of Old Town and new modern building.

Yerevan

Capital of Armenia, it is one of the world's oldest inhabited city. During the Soviet time, they tried to build a "perfect city". It is home to nearly I million people.

Zagreb

Capital of Croatia, more or less 800,000 people live there. Zagreb is a lovely city to walk around and discover new building.